"This book is a mine of wonderful reminders that we can go to God in honesty and vulnerability when we are overwhelmed by life."

— RUTH B. GRAHAM, author of *In Every Pew Sits a Broken Heart*

"To believe one does not matter, or is not loved, is tragedy. To understand that God loves and has not forgotten us, no matter our circumstances, is triumph. Marsha Maurer reminds those who despair that they need not."

— CAL THOMAS, syndicated columnist

"*With Healing Wings* is filled with prayers and scripture that help the reader cry out to the God of healing. Marsha Maurer's well chosen words create intimate conversations with the God of comfort. She guides her readers to a peaceful, hopeful place no matter the situation."

— CARMEN LEAL, author of *The Twenty- Third Psalm for Caregivers* and *The Twenty-Third Psalm for Those Who Grieve*

"When you are grasping for help and groping for words, *With Healing Wings* is the answer to prayers."

— THE REV. ERWIN WICHNER, U.S. Army Chaplain, retired; pastor, Zion Lutheran Church, Hillsboro, Oregon

With Healing Wings

With Healing Wings

Prayers *for* Those Who Hurt & Those Who Care

Marsha Maurer

Wings of blessing!
Marsha Maurer

LUCAS PARK BOOKS

ST. LOUIS, MISSOURI

ISBN Print: 9781603500357

Published by Lucas Park Books

www.lucasparkbooks.com

Contents

For those who hurt.
For those who help.
For those who hope.

For you who revere my name, the sun of righteousness
will rise with healing in its wings.
MALACHI 4:2

Those who hope in the LORD will renew their strength.
They will soar on wings like eagles.
ISAIAH 40:31

Because you are my help,
I sing in the shadow of your wings.
PSALM 63:7

He will cover you with his feathers,
and under his wings you will find refuge.
PSALM 91:4

Foreword

How can we endure the hardships of life that assail us? With the promise and power of prayer, we can not only survive but prevail. Unfortunately, in moments of distress, words often elude us.

With Healing Wings prompts conversation with God about the heartfelt concerns of those who suffer and those who care for them. Although caregivers will find their needs addressed in a separate section, many prayers may be prayed by both those hurting and those helping, or shared in one another's company. Additional prayers of thanksgiving acknowledge the blessing in adversity. Accompanying each prayer are God's own words of comfort, hope, and healing.

When we convey our heaviest burdens to God's throne of grace, He promises to respond *With Healing Wings*. He folds us close, feathered in His warm embrace—safe, secure, sheltered, and loved—transforming our personal needs into health and strength and joy.

Acknowledgments

With gratitude to my husband, Michael, for his loving support; to my sister Jolene Stackhouse, R.N., for her valuable assistance; to my sister Lesa Kendus, R.N.; to all my family for their devotion; to those who granted me the kind favor of endorsement; and to physicians, health care professionals, medical staff, clergy, friends, and all those who have so lovingly cared for, prayed for, and encouraged my family and me.

PRAYERS FOR HEALING

For Healing

Healing Lord,
    You have created me, know me, and love me. You have the power to make me prosper. No ailment or affliction, no disease or adversity, no pain or anguish is beyond Your cure. You took the suffering by the hand and healed them with a word or touch. Forgive my worry, my self-reliance, my doubt. Revive my confidence in You, and show me the wondrous miracle of Your healing. Amen.

Be merciful to me, LORD, for I am faint;
    O LORD, heal me, for my bones are in agony.
My soul is in anguish.
    How long, O LORD, how long?
Turn, O LORD, and deliver me;
    save me because of your unfailing love.
(PSALM 6:2–4)

Heal me, O LORD, and I will be healed;
    save me and I will be saved,
    for you are the one I praise. (JEREMIAH 17:14)

People brought all their sick to him and begged him to let the sick just touch the edge of his cloak, and all who touched him were healed. (MATTHEW 14:35b–36)

When the sun was setting, the people brought to Jesus all who had various kinds of sickness, and laying his hands on each one, he healed them. (LUKE 4:40)

The prayer offered in faith will make the sick person well. (JAMES 5:15a)

For Relief from Pain and Suffering

Lord of Relief,

I hurt, God, and the hurting won't stop. Remedies don't work, and relief won't come. I can't tolerate this pain much longer. Come to me with Your soothing Spirit. Place Your cool hand on my fevered brow. Quiet my writhing, and caress my clenched muscles. Loosen the knots in my stomach and thoughts. Soothe my frayed nerves, and slow my frantic heart. Assist the efforts of those who bring me relief. Remind me that You have known the terror of suffering, the cry for relief, and will not ask me to endure more than I can bear. Stay beside me till the hurting ends. Amen.

"Those who suffer he delivers in their suffering;
  he speaks to them in their affliction." (JOB 36:15)

For he has not despised or disdained
  the suffering of the afflicted one;
he has not hidden his face from him
  but has listened to his cry for help. (PSALM 22:24)

Have mercy on me, O God, have mercy on me,
  for in you my soul takes refuge.
I will take refuge in the shadow of your wings
  until the disaster has passed. (PSALM 57:1)

People brought to him all who were ill with various diseases, those suffering severe pain, the demon-possessed, those having seizures, and the paralyzed, and he healed them. (MATTHEW 4:24)

4

For Assurance of God's Presence

Abiding Lord,

I need to know that You are near, that You have not forgotten me. Assure me that Your eyes are ever watching, Your ears are ever listening, Your arms are ever outstretched. Reach for me. Touch me. Hold me close and tight. Enfold me in Your everlasting embrace. Comfort me with Your reassuring words and the warm breath of Your Spirit. In the drawing dark, abide with me. Amen.

The LORD's unfailing love
    surrounds the man who trusts in him. (PSALM 32:10)

"Then you will call, and the LORD will answer;
you will cry for help, and he will say: Here I am."
(ISAIAH 58:9)

They urged him strongly, "Stay with us, for it is nearly evening; the day is almost over." So he went in to stay with them. (LUKE 24:29)

Come near to God and he will come near to you. (James 4:8a)

For Help Praying

Listening Lord,

I can't seem to find the words. I don't even know what to say, except that I need Your help. You have invited me to bring any burden to You and have promised to respond. Recalling Your assurance and talking with You already ease my load. May I never doubt that You are hearing me, even anticipating my needs. Forgive me my self-sufficiency when our conversations have lapsed. Remind me to make time to speak with You often and to listen closely and patiently for Your certain reply. Amen.

"Ask and it will be given to you; seek and you will find; knock and the door will be opened to you. For everyone who asks receives; he who seeks finds; and to him who knocks, the door will be opened." (MATTHEW 7:7)

"If you remain in me and my words remain in you, ask whatever you wish, and it will be given you." (JOHN 15:7)

In the same way, the Spirit helps us in our weakness. We do not know what we ought to pray for, but the Spirit himself intercedes for us with groans that words cannot express. (ROMANS 8:26)

This is the confidence we have in approaching God: that if we ask anything according to his will, he hears us. And if we know that he hears us—whatever we ask—we know that we have what we asked of him. (1 JOHN 5:14–15)

For Accepting God's Will

Lord of Wisdom,

I have more questions than answers. I wonder why this is happening to me and what can be done. Help me to realize that there may not be answers to my questions and that solutions may not be the ones I want to hear. Forgive my stubborn insistence on my own desires. Show me that You will always send the best answers to my prayers, and that delayed relief may mean opportunity to exercise and strengthen my faith. Remind me that Your own Son recognized in His suffering Your plan for good. Reconcile me to limitation, and show me relief in surrender to Your perfect wisdom. Shift my focus from loss to growth, from resistance to resilience, from pity to perspective. Make me receptive to Your infinite grace. Amen.

"Your will be done
    on earth as it is in heaven." (MATTHEW 6:10b)

"Father, if you are willing, take this cup from me; yet not my will, but yours be done." (LUKE 22:42)

Jesus replied, "You do not realize now what I am doing, but later you will understand." (JOHN 13:7)

Oh, the depth of the riches of the wisdom and
        knowledge of God!
    How unsearchable his judgments,
    and his paths beyond tracing out! (ROMANS 11:33)

To Relinquish Control

Dependable Lord,

My vulnerability makes me uncomfortable. It forces me to realize that I am dispensable, to acknowledge my lack of control. Self-sufficiency is important to me; I am not accustomed to dependence. It is hard to see my dear ones assume responsibilities that I formerly handled so competently. I don't want to be a burden. Forgive my pride. Teach me to graciously accept help, to recognize that the loving ministry of others blesses each of us. Help me to specify the assistance I require and to request the gift of prayer. Remind me that I rely on You for all this world cannot supply. Make me confident in Your providence. Amen.

Trust in the LORD with all your heart
and lean not on your own understanding.
(PROVERBS 3:5)

"Be still, and know that I am God." (PSALM 46:10)

In his heart a man plans his course,
but the Lord determines his steps. (PROVERBS 16:9)

I lift up my eyes to the hills—
    where does my help come from?
My help comes from the LORD,
    the Maker of heaven and earth.
He will not let your foot slip—
    he who watches over you will not slumber;
indeed, he who watches over Israel
    will neither slumber nor sleep.
The LORD watches over you—
    the LORD is your shade at your right hand;
the sun will not harm you by day,
    nor the moon by night.
The LORD will keep you from all harm—
    he will watch over your life;
the LORD will watch over your coming and going
    both now and forevermore. (PSALM 121)

For Hope

Reliable Lord,
   Often I find it hard to imagine feeling better. Yet I know that hope animates healing. Nurture my reluctant optimism. Prompt me to continue advancing, confident in Your promises. Show me the certainty of Your blessing, that I may expect great goodness and anticipate victory. Stir my fervor with evidence of Your grace revealed. Amen.

"You will surely forget your trouble,
   recalling it only as waters gone by.
Life will be brighter than noonday,
   and darkness will become like morning.
You will be secure, because there is hope;
   you will look about you and take your rest in safety."
   (JOB 11:16–18)

We wait in hope for the LORD;
   he is our help and our shield.
In him our hearts rejoice,
   for we trust in his holy name.
May your unfailing love rest upon us, O LORD,
   even as we put our hope in you. (PSALM 33:20–22)

May the God of hope fill you with all joy and peace as
   you trust in him, so that you may overflow with hope
   by the power of the Holy Spirit. (ROMANS 15:13)

As the deer pants for streams of water,
    so my soul pants for you, O God.
My soul thirsts for God, for the living God…

Why are you downcast, O my soul?
    Why so disturbed within me?
Put your hope in God,
    for I will yet praise him,
    my Savior and my God. (PSALM 42:1–2a, 5)

For Strength

Lord of Strength,

How weak I feel. Can I summon the strength my healing requires? Support my body while it mends. Sustain and revive my flagging spirit. Encourage me in each small step of improvement to face the next, until I am functioning well again. Give me resilience to conquer the pain and setback that can accompany progress. Keep me determined and confident on my way to wellness. Make me tough, hardy, and strong. Fortify me with Your awesome power. Amen.

"The LORD is my strength and my song;
   he has become my salvation." (EXODUS 15:2a)

The LORD is my strength and my shield;
   my heart trusts in him, and I am helped.
My heart leaps for joy
   and I will give thanks to him in song. (PSALM 28:7)

"So do not fear, for I am with you;
   do not be dismayed, for I am your God.
I will strengthen you and help you;
   I will uphold you with my righteous right hand."
(ISAIAH 41:10)

For Endurance

Enduring Lord,
   I have been struggling so hard for so long. I feel drained and dispirited. I am losing strength and hope. Help me to go on, Lord. Keep me praying, even when I don't recognize Your response. Keep me trying, even when I am exhausted. Keep me calm, even when I fret. Keep me optimistic, even when I despair. Give me fortitude in the face of challenge, and help me to endure. Amen.

For everything that was written in the past was written to teach us, so that through endurance and the encouragement of Scriptures we might have hope. (ROMANS 15:4)

For God did not give us a spirit of timidity, but a spirit of power, of love and of self-discipline. (2 TIMOTHY 1:7)

For Energy

Invigorating Lord,
   Wrung out, done in, I feel too tired to lift even my voice to You. Shake me from this slump. Rouse me from exhaustion. Impel me to get going, mindful that expending energy fuels vitality. Activate my ambition. Give me enthusiasm for my goals and stamina to pursue them. Revive my frail faith; refresh my flagging spirit; restore my vigor. Amen.

"The Lord will guide you always; he will satisfy your needs in a sun-scorched land and will strengthen your frame. You will be like a well-watered garden, like a spring whose waters never fail." (Isaiah 58:11)

I can do everything through him who gives me strength. (Philippians 4:13)

For Appetite

Bread of Heaven,

Although I need to eat to sustain my health, the look, the smell, the taste of food have lost their appeal. Restore my appetite, and give me a taste for wholesome fare. Nourish my body and soul with the bread of Your hand. Make me hunger for Your salutary provisions. Amen.

Taste and see that the LORD is good;
    blessed is the man who takes refuge in him.
(PSALM 34:8)

The eyes of all look to you,
    and you give them their food at the proper time.
You open your hand
    and satisfy the desires of every living thing.
(PSALM 145:15–16)

Then Jesus declared, "I am the bread of life. He who comes to me will never go hungry, and he who believes in me will never be thirsty." (JOHN 6:35)

For Sleep

Lord of Rest,

Eyes wide, thoughts churning, fears raging, I toss
and turn and flail about. Sleep eludes me. Reveal Your
presence in the sterling stars of inky night. Cradle me;
pillow me. Quiet me; cover me. Nestle me; still me.
Soothe me with the vigil of Your Spirit and the lullaby
rush of Your wings. Tuck the twisted sheets about me,
whisper assurances of Your nearness, and blanket me
with sleep. Amen.

I will lie down and sleep in peace,
   for you alone, O LORD,
      make me dwell in safety. (PSALM 4:8)

He grants sleep to those he loves. (PSALM 127:2b)

"Come to me, all you who are weary and burdened, and I
will give you rest." (MATTHEW 11:28)

In Anxiety

Calming Lord,

The winds of worry howl about me. I feel anxious, tense, and uneasy. Concerns assail me. Answers elude me. Fears batter me. Restless and disturbed, I yearn for relief. Still the storms that lash at me. Soothe my troubled heart. Ease my teeming thoughts. Relax my taut nerves. Quell my anxiety. Let me feel the serenity of Your tranquil presence, the hush of Your quiet voice, the calm of Your gentle guidance. Grant me peace. Amen.

Do not be anxious about anything, but in everything, by prayer and petition, with thanksgiving, present your requests to God. And the peace of God, which transcends all understanding, will guard your hearts and your minds in Christ Jesus. (PHILIPPIANS 4:6–7)

Cast all your anxiety on him because he cares for you. (1 PETER 5:7)

In Sadness

Lord of Cheer,

Crying comes and goes, but sadness remains. My tears and agony exhaust me. The future looks bleak. I sorrow to the point of despair. How will I ever overcome this misery and find the will to go on? I can't imagine now that life will ever look bright, that I will ever find cheer a companion again. Remind me of Your response to the psalmist who cried to You, groaning and weeping. Even in his depths, You gave him strength to survive and restored him to joy. Banish my gloom, and let glad glimpses begin my return to happiness. Deliver me to delight. Amen.

"I have heard your prayer and seen your tears;
I will heal you." (2 Kings 20:5b)

"I am worn out from groaning;
    all night long I flood my bed with weeping
    and drench my couch with tears…
The Lord has heard my cry for mercy;
    the Lord accepts my prayer." (Psalm 6:6, 9)

You turned my wailing into dancing;
    you removed my sackcloth and clothed me with joy,
that my heart may sing to you and not be silent.
    O Lord my God, I will give you thanks forever.
(Psalm 30:11–12)

Let me hear joy and gladness;
  let the bones you have crushed rejoice. (Psalm 51:8)

"Blessed are you who weep now,
  for you will laugh." (Luke 6:21b)

When Fearful

Valiant Lord,

Can You feel my trembling? I dread the unknown and shrink from what lies ahead. What is next? Will it help? Will it hurt? Can I cope? I am tense, nervous, uneasy, though I try not to show my fear. Yet keeping a strong facade is difficult, too. Well-intentioned palliatives do little to soothe me. I know the reasons I should be confident, but my qualms are not eased by rational assurances. Relieve my apprehension. Quiet my quivering. Reassure me that You will not require more than I can bear, and that You will strengthen me for any challenge. Give me courage to withstand. Make me bold and unflinching, calm and sure. Amen.

I sought the LORD, and he answered me;
   he delivered me from all my fears. (PSALM 34:4)

"Surely God is my salvation;
   I will trust and not be afraid." (ISAIAH 12:2)

Strengthen the feeble hands,
   steady the knees that give way;
say to those with fearful hearts,
   "Be strong, do not fear;
your God will come." (ISAIAH 35:3–4)

For I am convinced that neither death nor life, neither angels nor demons, neither the present nor the future, nor any powers, neither height nor depth, nor anything else in all creation, will be able to separate us from the love of God that is in Christ Jesus our Lord. (Romans 8:38–39)

When Irritable or Angry

Good Lord,

Adversity has shrunken my life. I chafe beneath the demands and disruptions of this burden. I feel betrayed and angry. Shift my focus from this consuming pain and pity. In my struggle, when life does not seem fair, demonstrate Your power to change me. Renew my attitude. Help me to seek the positive, though I cannot now imagine it. May Your inspiration enrich my life and edify others. Transform hardship into healing, oppression into opportunity, bitterness into blessing. Prepare me to receive Your overflowing grace. Amen.

Do not conform any longer to the pattern of this world, but be transformed by the renewing of your mind. Then you will be able to test and approve what God's will is— his good, pleasing, and perfect will. (ROMANS 12:2)

Finally, brothers, whatever is true, whatever is noble, whatever is right, whatever is pure, whatever is lovely, whatever is admirable—if anything is excellent or praiseworthy—think about such things. (PHILIPPIANS 4:8)

When Overwhelmed

Triumphant Lord,

I'm sorry, but this burden is entirely too hard to handle, too much to endure. I am overwhelmed by demands I cannot meet, difficulties I cannot face, the need for strength I do not have. I wonder why You have abandoned me. Where will I find the reserves to tackle these insurmountable problems? When You found suffering unbearable, You sought the help of Your Father. Remind me by Your example to go to Him often—to search His Word and reach out in prayer. Teach me how to break my challenges into manageable tasks. Give me the resources required to conquer. Show me success. Turn my desperation into triumph. Amen.

I call to God,
    and the LORD saves me.
Evening, morning, and noon
    I cry out in distress,
and he hears my voice. (PSALM 55:16–17)

Cast your cares on the LORD
    and he will sustain you. (PSALM 55:22)

Now to him who is able to do immeasurably more than all we ask or imagine, according to his power that is at work within us, to him be glory in the church and in Christ Jesus throughout all generations, for ever and ever! Amen. (EPHESIANS 3:20–21)

In Weariness

Sustaining Lord,

A dreary lassitude creeps over me. How weary I am. Exhausted from problems, restricted by limitations, sluggish with inactivity, I have lost interest. The further I sink into lethargy, the more difficult it becomes to rise from these doldrums. Extend Your hand to lift me from my languor and apathy. Encourage me to try. Show me the benefit of even small efforts to appreciate and enlarge my shrunken world. Expand my engagement in the here and now. Invest the tedious, mundane, and difficult with holiness. Restore my vitality, and revive my enthusiasm for living. Amen.

Do you not know?
Have you not heard?
The LORD is the everlasting God,
the Creator of the ends of the earth.
He will not grow tired or weary,
and his understanding no one can fathom.
He gives strength to the weary
and increases the power of the weak.
Even youths grow tired and weary,
and young men stumble and fall;
but those who hope in the LORD
will renew their strength.
They will soar on wings like eagles;
they will run and not grow weary,
they will walk and not be faint. (ISAIAH 40:28–31)

"My grace is sufficient for you, for my power is made perfect in weakness." (2 CORINTHIANS 12:9)

In Loneliness

My Dear Lord,

I feel lonely and forlorn. No one seems to understand what I am going through. I bear my burdens alone. I doubt that anyone cares. Even when I want to join in, my sense of alienation keeps me from feeling fully engaged. I withdraw because participating is more bother than pleasure. Any attempt at all seems like effort. Isolation is easier.

I need Your help to break this solitary cycle. Help me to reach out to others, even though it may be painful initially. Shift my focus from myself to a genuine interest in others. Let me seek ways to connect. Give me the impetus and desire to extend myself. Show me that the best way to overcome self-doubt and pity is to reach a hand to others. Help me to see that by risking a little, I stand to gain a lot. Remind me that You, too, felt rejected and misunderstood. May I feel Your presence and power. Amen.

For he will deliver the needy who cry out,
    the afflicted who have no one to help. (PSALM 72:12)

God has said,
"Never will I leave you;
    never will I forsake you." (HEBREWS 13:5)

In Disappointment

Uplifting Lord,

Disappointment is swallowing me. I feel the frustration of setback and arrested ambition, the regret of poor choice and lost opportunity, the failure of unmet expectation and unfulfilled potential. Keep my disappointment from turning to anger, affecting relationships, and consuming me. Forgive my self-centered preoccupation with all that is wrong. Focus my attention on all that is right—on goodness, success, and blessing. Dispel my bitterness and gloom. Help me to cultivate contentment. Satisfy me with the irrepressible largess of Your Spirit. Amen.

Praise the LORD, O my soul;
    and forget not all his benefits—
who forgives all your sins
    and heals all your diseases,
who redeems your life from the pit
    and crowns you with love and compassion,
who satisfies your desires with good things,
    so that your youth is renewed like the eagle's.
(PSALM 103:2–5)

In Discouragement

Encouraging Lord,
　　I feel dejected, depressed, discouraged. Progress has stalled. Promise has dimmed. I need to find the will to go on. Show me the potential that has faded from my sight. Spur me with reason to persevere. Hearten me with Your word, Your response to prayer, and Your ambassadors who care for me. Make me fervent in my effort and bold in my struggle. Give me grit, and pluck, and heart. Buoyed by Your power, may I not only persist, but prevail. Amen.

"Be strong and courageous. Do not be terrified; do not be discouraged, for the LORD your God will be with you wherever you go." (JOSHUA 1:9)

Yet I am always with you;
　　you hold me by my right hand.
You guide me with your counsel,
　　and afterward you will take me into glory.
(PSALM 73:23–24)

In Trouble

Lord of Refuge and Strength,

I have tumbled into trouble and cannot extract myself. Prospects look murky, and I am not sure which direction is up. I am confounded by my circumstances, tormented with uncertainty. Lift me from my misery, and show me Your succor. Lead me to identify prospects and carefully evaluate options in finding the best way toward light. Encourage me in each small step. Manifest Your presence, and reveal Your path. Amen.

———————

The LORD is a refuge for the oppressed,
a stronghold in times of trouble.
Those who know your name will trust in you,
for you, LORD, have never forsaken those who seek
you. (PSALM 9:9–10)

You are my hiding place;
you will protect me from trouble
and surround me with songs of deliverance.
(PSALM 32:7)

Is any one of you in trouble? He should pray.
(JAMES 5:13)

In the day of my trouble I will call to you,
for you will answer me. (PSALM 86:7)

"In this world you will have trouble. But take heart! I have overcome the world." (JOHN 16:33b)

In Loss

Lord of All Fullness,

I have an empty ache inside. Loss crushes my spirit. I feel angry, sad, numb, fearful, lonely, vulnerable, and tired. You seem far away. Remind me that recovery takes time. Help me to work at my own pace through the "whys" and "ifs," to confront the pain and face the longing for what is gone. Comfort me with joyous memories that always will endure. Use my loss to clarify the truth, beauty, and love that are most essential and significant. May I embrace compassion offered and possibilities ahead to grow closer to others and to You in wisdom, strength, and love. Amen.

———————————

"The eternal God is your refuge, and underneath are the everlasting arms." (DEUTERONOMY 33:27)

He heals the brokenhearted
and binds up their wounds. (PSALM 147:3)

In a Troubled Relationship

Lord of Love,

I find it hard to reconcile my battered relationship. Faults and grudges block my willingness to see redeeming virtues. Help me to find a loving approach to resolve our difficulties and bridge our differences. May I recognize my own guilt in our division. Forgive my stubborn selfishness, and make me willing to compromise. Replace my criticism with kindness. Give me forbearance to overlook disagreement, betrayal, and neglect. Show me how to begin the difficult task of forgiving. Dissolve our rancor. Mend our antagonism and indifference. Help us to listen carefully and affirm each other, to realize our shared blessing, to cultivate mutual respect. Make us understanding and generous. Restore harmony, and nurture our love. Amen.

"This is my command: Love each other." (JOHN 15:17)

Love must be sincere. Hate what is evil; cling to what is good. Be devoted to one another in brotherly love. Honor one another above yourselves. (ROMANS 12:9–10)

Love is patient, love is kind. It does not envy, it does not boast, it is not proud. It is not rude, it is not self-seeking, it is not easily angered, it keeps no record of wrongs. Love does not delight in evil but rejoices with the truth. It always protects, always trusts, always hopes, always perseveres. (1 CORINTHIANS 13:4–7)

Therefore, as God's chosen people, holy and dearly loved, clothe yourselves with compassion, kindness, humility, gentleness and patience. Bear with each other and forgive whatever grievances you may have against one another. Forgive as the Lord forgave you. (COLOSSIANS 3:12–13)

For Peace

Lord of Peace,

   The turmoil in my mind has seeped into my whole being. Assailed by the unpredictable and uncontrollable, I cannot shake my tremulous thoughts. Over and over they replay, wearing an inescapable rut. Help me to dismiss these incessant and unsettling agonies. Dispel the brooding and fidgeting that nettle and torment me. Turn Your face to me, and displace my anguish with Your radiant serenity. Amen.

"The LORD bless you
   and keep you;
the LORD make his face shine upon you
   and be gracious to you;
the LORD turn his face toward you
   and give you peace." (NUMBERS 6:24–26)

A heart at peace gives life to the body. (PROVERBS 14:30a)

"Peace I leave with you; my peace I give you. I do not give to you as the world gives. Do not let your hearts be troubled and do not be afraid." (JOHN 14:27)

For Comfort

My Good Shepherd,
Walk beside me and assure me that there is nothing
I need that You cannot provide. Quench my thirst for
respite, and give ease to my weary heart. Solace me with
assurance of Your vigilant guidance. Nourish me with
Your tender love, and bring me safely home. Amen.

The Lord is my shepherd; I shall not want.
He maketh me to lie down in green pastures: he
leadeth me beside the still waters.
He restoreth my soul: he leadeth me in the paths of
righteousness for his name's sake.
Yea, though I walk through the valley of the shadow
of death, I will fear no evil: for thou art with me; thy rod
and thy staff they comfort me.
Thou preparest a table before me in the presence of
mine enemies: thou anointest my head with oil; my cup
runneth over.
Surely goodness and mercy shall follow me all the
days of my life: and I will dwell in the house of the Lord
for ever. (Psalm 23, KJV)

For Patience

Patient Lord,

You always have time for us, Lord, and never hurry.
While living on this earth, You took the time to listen to
human needs and to ponder Your Father's design. Show
me, by Your example, the blessings in an easy tempo.
When I am frustrated with the delay of healing, show me
in this time of suspended activity, the merit of moments,
the pleasure of relationships, the solace of visits with You.
Let me listen closely to what suffering can teach me. Give
me reverence for what is spiritually essential. As I return
to health, remind me to savor the gifts of a slower pace.
May I be measured in living, deliberate in enterprise,
serene in disposition, and receptive to unexpected riches.
Amen.

Wait for the LORD;
> be strong and take heart
> and wait for the LORD. (PSALM 27:14)

I wait for the LORD, my soul waits,
> and in his word I put my hope. (PSALM 130:5)

Be joyful in hope, patient in affliction, faithful in prayer.
(ROMANS 12:12)

For Deliverance from Despair

Lord of Deliverance,
Despair sits heavily upon me, crushing my very breath. My body droops beneath the oppressive burden. My mind groans, my spirit slumps, my will withers. I have lost my desire to go on. Raise me from these depths, Dear Lord. Help me to sit back in my chair, draw the deep breath of Your reviving Spirit, rise slowly on my wobbling resolve, plant my feet firmly in Your promises, and step forward yet again. Hearten my efforts to persevere. Encourage me to confront my challenges with renewed vigor, and let me feel again the pulsing warmth of joy. Amen.

Out of the depths I cry to you, O LORD;
O Lord, hear my voice.
Let your ears be attentive
to my cry for mercy. (PSALM 130:1–2)

Though you have made me see troubles, many
and bitter,
you will restore my life again;
from the depths of the earth
you will again bring me up. (PSALM 71:20)

We are hard pressed on every side, but not crushed; perplexed, but not in despair; persecuted, but not abandoned; struck down, but not destroyed. We always carry around in our body the death of Jesus, so that the life of Jesus may also be revealed in our body.
(2 CORINTHIANS 4:8–10)

My life is consumed by anguish
  and my years by groaning;
my strength fails because of my affliction,
  and my bones grow weak…
But I trust in you, O LORD;
  I say, "You are my God."…
Let your face shine on your servant;
  save me in your unfailing love…
Be strong and take heart,
  all you who hope in the LORD.
(PSALM 31:10, 14, 16, 24)

For Perseverance

Devoted Lord,

I expected a few stumbles in life, but I didn't know I would fall so often, or so hard, or hurt so much. I didn't know that picking myself up would be so difficult. Removing one obstacle seems to reveal others. Give me perseverance in this trail of trials. Help me to face life's impediments as they arise, not worrying about those ahead or dwelling on those behind. Help me to recognize opportunity in the paths You open for me. Assure me that You will provide strength for the moment and wisdom for the way. Accompany me on this precarious road heavenward. Amen.

Blessed is the man who perseveres under trial, because when he has stood the test, he will receive the crown of life that God has promised to those who love him. (JAMES 1:12)

We also rejoice in our suffering, because we know that suffering produces perseverance; perseverance, character; and character, hope. And hope does not disappoint us, because God has poured out his love into our hearts by the Holy Spirit, whom he has given us. (ROMANS 5:3–5)

For Joy

Lord of Joy,

It isn't easy to be happy just now. Demands on my health and attention diminish my spirit. Pleasure eludes me. Rekindle in me a glimmer of gladness. Remind me that the light of happiness cannot be found as the object of my search, but carried within, its glow will illumine all I encounter. Even in these murky moments, may I shine with contentment, that my spark of joy may light the lamps of those it reaches. Disposition is a conscious choice, which quickly becomes habit. Teach me the talent of play. Remind me that to share Your fullness of joy, I must be generous of myself. May I blaze with Your incandescent love. Show me that when I feel least cheerful, a smile on my lips, a gleam in my eye, and a song in my voice can dispel the dark and invite delight. Amen.

Let all who take refuge in you be glad;
>   let them ever sing for joy. (PSALM 5:11)

A cheerful look brings joy to the heart,
>   and good news gives health to the bones.
(PROVERBS 15:30)

Be joyful always; pray continually; give thanks in all circumstances, for this is God's will for you in Christ Jesus. (1 THESSALONIANS 5:16)

For Help

Benevolent Lord,
　　Wrestling with my challenges, I feel hopeless in the struggle. I need Your help. Give me vision to see how to proceed and humility to accept assistance. Help me to recognize the help You provide. May I take the proffered hand, the opportunity presented. Make my will and competence sufficient to tackle the tasks before me. Crown my efforts with success that others may see and glorify the work of Your benevolent hands. Amen.

God is our refuge and strength,
　　an ever present help in trouble.
Therefore we will not fear. (PSALM 46:1–2a)

Call upon me in the day of trouble;
　　I will deliver you, and you will honor me.
(PSALM 50:15)

"Because he loves me," says the LORD, "I will rescue him;
　　I will protect him, for he acknowledges my name.
He will call upon me, and I will answer him;
　　I will be with him in trouble,
　　I will deliver him and honor him." (PSALM 91:14–15)

For Confidence

Bold Lord,

How mutable and unruly life is. Just when I think I am in control, the ground beneath my feet shifts again. Certain though I am of uncertainty, my fear of the unpredictable persists. My struggle to resist life's vicissitudes fuels my panic and dread. I lose confidence. Let me surrender my attempts to control, acknowledging my dependence on Your loving omniscience. Embolden me with the surety of Your promise and power, that I may confront my qualms and proceed in the face of them. Hearten me with a sanguine spirit and great expectation. Amen.

"With God all things are possible." (MATTHEW 19:26b)

Let us then approach the throne of grace with confidence, so that we may receive mercy and find grace to help us in our time of need. (HEBREWS 4:16)

For a Sense of Humor

Lord of Laughter,
   Each day needs some of the sublime and the
ridiculous. Just now I suffer from a dearth of mirth. Pour
me an elixir of levity, some merry medicine. Loosen my
stiff-necked ways, relax my rigid outlook, limber my
seriousness. Give me a supple soul and a lithe spirit.
Transform grim to grin, for there is little amusement in
the grave. Bless me with bliss. Reveal the oblation in
laughter, the sacrament in a smile. May my spirit soar in
an exaltation of larks. Amen.

Pleasant words are a honeycomb,
   sweet to the soul and healing to the bones.
(PROVERBS 16:24)

A cheerful heart is good medicine. (PROVERBS 17:22a)

For Grace

Gracious Lord,

Each day, each moment, blessings from Your bountiful hand cascade my way.

Why do I so seldom feel Your abundance breezing in, Your sanctifying showers and the refreshing respite they bring? Make my parched spirit receptive to Your extravagant grace. Show me that those delusions of relief I seek are only mirage. Drench the desert of my soul with Your excellent mercy. And in my resultant growth, make me more grateful, more discerning, more generous, more holy. Amen.

Delight yourself in the LORD
    and he will give you the desires of your heart.
(PSALM 37:4)

I love the LORD, for he heard my voice;
    he heard my cry for mercy.
Because he turned his ear to me,
    I will call on him as long as I live. (PSALM 116:1–2)

And God is able to make all grace abound to you, so that in all things at all times, having all that you need, you will abound in every good work. (2 CORINTHIANS 9:8)

For it is by grace you have been saved, through faith— and this not from yourselves, it is the gift of God. (EPHESIANS 2:8)

For Faith

Faithful Lord,

When I try to understand Your love, I am confounded. My mind cannot capture the mystery of Your grace. Simple belief is not easy. Faith means abandoning dependence on my own reason and competence. Faith means facing human failure, discomfort, and demise. Faith means turning to Your power to transform hurt and guilt into health and wholeness. Help me to resolve my doubt by relinquishing rational limits to the unfathomable certainty of Your promises fulfilled. Amen.

I trust in your unfailing love;
    my heart rejoices in your salvation.
I will sing to the LORD,
    for he has been good to me. (PSALM 13:5–6)

Jesus turned and saw her. "Take heart, daughter," he said, "your faith has healed you." And the woman was healed from that moment. (MATTHEW 9:22)

"Everything is possible for him who believes." (MARK 9:23b)

Now faith is being sure of what we hope for and certain of what we do not see. (HEBREWS 11:1)

For Forgiveness

My Redeemer,

Relieve this burden of sin and guilt that weighs upon me. Forgive my impatience with myself and others, my inordinate expectations, my hurtful words, my icy neglect, my careless anger. Forgive my thoughtless grumbling, my greedy envy, my selfish pride. Teach me to be less critical, more forgiving; less demanding, more generous. Help me to live renewed by Your goodness. Thank You for Your great mercy, freely given, redeeming me from this tainted transience to that perfect eternity with You. Amen.

Create in me a pure heart, O God,
    and renew a steadfast spirit within me. (PSALM 51:10)

In him we have redemption through his blood, the forgiveness of sins, in accordance with the riches of God's grace that he lavished on us with all wisdom and understanding. (EPHESIANS 1:7–8)

For he has rescued us from the dominion of darkness and brought us into the kingdom of the Son he loves, in whom we have redemption, the forgiveness of sins. (COLOSSIANS 1:13–14)

If we confess our sins, he is faithful and just and will forgive us our sins and purify us from all unrighteousness. (1 JOHN 1:9)

Facing Decision

Divine Counselor,

My choices challenge me. I veer from one alternative to another. Keep me from becoming overwhelmed by options. Lead me to the sources I need to gather reliable and useful information. Let me ask appropriate questions and listen attentively to advice. Assist me in weighing issues, considering circumstances, and contemplating effects. Encourage me to consult Your wisdom and seek the prayers of others. Show me the best decision for me and for those I love. Amen.

I will instruct you and teach you in the way you
    should go;
  I will counsel you and watch over you. (Psalm 32:8)

"For I know the plans I have for you," declares the Lord, "plans to prosper you and not to harm you, plans to give you hope and a future." (Jeremiah 29:11)

Before Tests

Omniscient Lord,

I don't know what is wrong with me. I pray that the tests I am about to undergo will reveal the problem and suggest a solution. Make me relaxed and comfortable for the procedures. May the testing, reading, and diagnosis be performed with skill and care. Give those attending to me the wisdom to detect the nature of my malady, to establish its cause, and to discern an effective remedy. Through their endeavors, display Your love for me. Amen.

I call on you, O God, for you will answer me;
    give ear to me and hear my prayer.
Show the wonder of your great love. (PSALM 17:6–7a)

"He gives wisdom to the wise
    and knowledge to the discerning.
He reveals deep and hidden things;
    he know what lies in darkness,
    and light dwells with him." (DANIEL 2:21b–22)

Before Surgery

Lord of Refuge,
   Bless the hands of those who tend and mend me.
When the intricacies of procedures are demanding, make
them focused and confident. When the bustle of their
labors is unsettling, make them calm and steady. When
the insistence of time pressures them, make them alert
and aware. When consequential decisions arise, make
them swift and sure. Thank You for their knowledge,
training, and talent in the healing arts. Guide their efforts,
and grant me a comfortable, prompt, and favorable
recovery. Amen.

"The eternal God is your refuge,
   and underneath are the everlasting arms."
(DEUTERONOMY 33:27)

The LORD will keep you from all harm—he will watch
over your life. (PSALM 121:7)

47

Before Therapy

Steadfast Lord,

Strengthen me in this therapy to stretch and strive toward improvement. Thank You for my dedicated therapists. Assist us in setting challenging, yet attainable, goals. Make me persistent and determined. Animate my efforts with evidence of progress that I may grow steadily more capable. When rehabilitation becomes arduous and tiresome, encourage me. Move me steadfastly forward. Amen.

And we know that in all things God works for the good of those who love him, who have been called according to his purpose. (ROMANS 8:28)

Before Treatment

Lord of Promise,
  Prepare me for the treatment I am about to undergo. Make me calm and receptive to healing. Keep my expectations realistic. Help me to accept that the healing You send may differ from the version of wellness I hope for. Bless the hands of those who administer my treatment that it may work to restore my health. Amen.

The LORD is good to all;
  he has compassion on all he has made. (PSALM 145:9)

"All things are possible with God." (MARK 10:27b)

In Impairment

Renewing Lord,

I never thought I would have to face this impairment.
And now I realize that I cannot turn back time nor change
the future. I mourn my loss, and I fear that my strength
may be insufficient for the challenges my debilitation
demands. May I recognize that not all things can be fixed,
that my prospects may not fit my narrow expectations.
Help me to see this disruption not as devastation, but
as redirection. Renew my reliance on You. Show me
my capability, fortify my will, and rally my spirit in my
efforts toward rehabilitation. Make me confident in a
brighter tomorrow. Amen.

You hear, O LORD, the desire of the afflicted;
    you encourage them, and you listen to their cry.
(PSALM 10:17)

The LORD is faithful to all his promises
    and loving toward all he has made.
The LORD upholds all whose who fall
    and lifts up all who are bowed down.
(PSALM 145:13b–14)

Facing Terminal Illness

Lord of Life,

Death, which seemed so far away, is suddenly uncomfortably near. I am angry at curtailed opportunities. I regret my abbreviated days. I am frustrated by my inability to arrest my accelerated end. Help me to recognize that my fear, anger, and denial are all normal responses. May my loved ones have the grace to understand that these expressions are not directed at them, so that our remaining time together is a blessing to be shared. Give me an appreciation for all the gifts of this world and a readiness for the world to come. Show me how to accept and face my fear to release its grip on me. Make me comfortable in my demise. May I persevere with peaceful courage, confident in Your promise of eternal life. Amen.

Jesus said to her, "I am the resurrection and the life. He who believes in me will live, even though he dies; and whoever lives and believes in me will never die." (JOHN 11:25–26)

In all these things we are more than conquerors through him who loved us. (ROMANS 8:37)

In Declining Health

Eternal Lord,

I know my health is waning. Give me grace to handle the unfamiliar and uneasy future. Help me to recognize that my dwindling condition does not mean diminishing hope. Though my physical vigor is decreasing, You keep me strong in faith and sure in my heavenly goal. You have conquered the relentless ravaging of time and share Your victory with me. Assure me that when my flesh and blood fail, You will take me home. May I begin to know that peace which You will fully reveal to me in paradise. Amen.

But I trust in you, O LORD;
I say, "You are my God."
My times are in your hands. (PSALM 31:14–15a)

Therefore we do not lose heart. Though outwardly we are wasting away, yet inwardly we are being renewed day by day. For our light and momentary troubles are achieving for us an eternal glory that far outweighs them all. So we fix our eyes not on what is seen, but on what is unseen. For what is seen is temporary, but what is unseen is eternal. (2 CORINTHIANS 4:16–18)

As Aging

Lord of Hope,

    I hoped to live long, yet I am surprised to grow old so quickly. As my years accumulate, I struggle with the challenges of declining energy and strength, of slower limbs and wits, of precarious health. Yet despite diminished faculty and facility, I praise You that I retain what I need most, Your love and promise of salvation. With this assurance, I can face the limits of impairment and dependence, the loss of dear ones, the disturbance of change. Give me purpose, bravery, enthusiasm, and cheer. Assuage my frustration, and forgive my complaint. Make me patient in adversity, positive in attitude, persistent in hope. May I never abandon my effort, but incline always onward, upward, and nearer to You. Amen.

I was young and now I am old,
    yet I have never seen the righteous forsaken.
(Psalm 37:25a)

"Even to your old age and gray hairs
    I am he, I am he who will sustain you.
I have made you and I will carry you;
    I will sustain you and I will rescue you."
(Isaiah 46:4)

Approaching Death

Lord of Glory,

I know that my time here on earth is nearly over. Thank You for Your abundant blessings in my life and for claiming me as Your own. You have seen me this far; assure me that You will stay by my side to see me through. In the brief moments remaining with my dear ones, may we cherish each other and reflect on the gift of love we share. When I am gone, soothe my survivors with the healing balm of time and Your comforting assurance of our reunion. Though my body perishes, banish my fear with the blissful promise of paradise, which You have prepared for me. Expectant and welcoming, may I enter a life of greater love, greater wisdom, greater joy, and greater peace. Sanctify me, and bear me tenderly into Your glorious company. With my final sigh, may I inhale the breath of Your Spirit. Amen.

Into your hands I commit my spirit. (PSALM 31:5a)

Praise be to the God and Father of our Lord Jesus Christ! In his great mercy he has given us new birth into a living hope through the resurrection of Jesus Christ from the dead, and into an inheritance that can never perish, spoil or fade—kept in heaven for you. (1 PETER 1:3–4)

Jesus said to her, "I am the resurrection and the life. He who believes in me will live, even though he dies; and whoever lives and believes in me will never die." (JOHN 11:25–26)

Seeking Heaven

Lord,

I have never prayed much. In fact, I haven't had much time for You or religion. I haven't really given much thought to what happens after I die. I have always thought that fully living life in this world would be enough. Now I'm not so sure. I can't imagine this is all there is. I'd like to think that there is more somehow. I'm not completely satisfied, and I'm a little fearful. But, it's probably too late now. I haven't lived a perfect life; sometimes I've made mistakes and hurt people. Now I wonder if there really is a heaven, if I've lived a good enough life, and if I might still be able to go there.

You have said in the Bible that I cannot earn heaven, that instead You have given a free gift, no strings attached. You sent Your only Son Jesus to die for the sins of all the world, to redeem us. All we have to do is believe that Jesus is the Savior and accept His forgiveness in order to claim heaven. That seems rather unbelievable. Who would make such a painful sacrifice? Who could have so much love? Help me to see that I cannot measure Your mercy by my human understanding. I must be able to give myself over to You, to admit my sins, to ask for forgiveness, and to trust fully in Your promise. Give me faith that You will forgive my sins, redeem me, and take me to heaven. Amen.

"For God so loved the world that he gave his one and only Son, that whoever believes in him shall not perish but have eternal life." (JOHN 3:16)

To Confess Faith

Lord,

I am ready to accept Jesus as my Savior. I believe that You have created me and that You sent Your Son Jesus to die for me, to redeem me from sin, and to restore me as Your own. Forgive all my sins. Send Your Holy Spirit into my heart, and renew my life that I may live as You would have me live. And when I die, take me to heaven to live with You forever. Amen.

If you confess with your mouth, "Jesus is Lord," and believe in your heart that God raised him from the dead, you will be saved. (ROMANS 10:9)

PRAYERS OF THANKSGIVING

Thanks for Health Care Workers

Lord of Labors,

So many efforts combine to make health care efficient, effective, and caring. Bless all who work to support and deliver health care in a myriad of ways—those who aid in emergency; transport the ill; keep records; manage facilities; perform tests; clean spills; wash laundry; cook meals; maintain equipment; administer anesthesia, treatment, and therapy; and offer countless other services. We appreciate their industry, diligence, and dedication to endeavors that are not always visible, recognized, or rewarded. Give them satisfaction in their duties and joy in their charges that their valuable contributions to healing may glorify You. Amen.

"Whatever you did for one of the least of these brothers of mine, you did for me." (MATTHEW 25:40b)

Thanks for Physicians

Divine Physician,

Thank You for those physicians who direct my care, the conduits and facilitators of Your healing power. Their knowledge and skill are a sacred trust from Your own hands. May they administer this charge carefully, compassionately, respectfully. Sharpen their senses. Bless them with a sensitive touch and a discerning eye. Make them listen attentively to both words and silences. Provide the stamina, enthusiasm, and mental acuity they need for their demanding work. May they honor the confidence of those whom they serve. Never let them lose reverence for the wonder of Your healing. Amen.

"I was sick and you looked after me." (MATTHEW 25:36b)

Thanks for Nurses

Lord of Grace,
   Thank You for the nurses who minister to my needs
with compassion and cheer. They are Your voice, Your
hands, Your presence at the side of the ill and suffering.
They respond to my unexpressed fears and never grow
weary of my questions. They allay my concerns, relieve
my suffering, hearten my outlook. Their skilled treatment
and caring demeanor prompt my recovery. Remind them
of the importance of their noble calling. The knowledge
and support of many enable their efforts, but they are
the ones at my side, hearing, touching, and reassuring
me. Encourage them when they are pressured and
discouraged. Send more people into this challenging and
rewarding field. Thank You for the blessing of their grace.
Amen.

Blessed is he who has regard for the weak. (PSALM 41:1a)

Thanks for Medical Advancements

Wondrous Lord,

Thank You for the healing effectiveness of medicines and drugs, the chemists who develop them, the companies that distribute them, the pharmacists who dispense them. Thank You for advancements in medical technology and those who design equipment to aid in diagnosis and treatment. Thank You for the machines, materials, and procedures used to repair, renew, and restore. Thank You for the intellect, creativity, and dedication of those behind the scenes who facilitate functioning of the amazing human body You have created. May these advancements improve lives to Your glory. Amen.

You are great and do marvelous deeds;
    you alone are God. (PSALM 86:10)

Give thanks to the LORD for his unfailing love
    and his wonderful deeds for men. (PSALM 107:8)

Thanks for Help

Merciful Lord,

Before I asked, You knew the help I needed. You knew what was best for me. Thank You for Your compassion, for Your comfort, for Your help. Thank You for all I have discovered in the demands You have made of me, for strengthening my faith in my reliance on You. Thank You for showing me the way, bringing me by the hand, and delivering me safely. May I be tireless in gratitude to You. Amen.

The LORD is gracious and righteous;
  our God is full of compassion.
The LORD protects the simplehearted;
  when I was in great need, he saved me.
Be at rest once more, O my soul,
  for the LORD has been good to you. (PSALM 116:5–7)

Now to him who is able to do immeasurably more than all we ask or imagine, according to his power that is at work within us, to him be glory in the church and in Christ Jesus throughout all generations, for ever and ever! Amen. (EPHESIANS 3:20–21)

63

Thanks for Healing

My Great Maker,

   Praise to You who have heard my prayers and healed me. You have calmed my worries, assuaged my anguish, banished my fears. You have restored my body, raised my spirit, and renewed my vigor. Remind me that in You all things are possible. Thank You for Your salutary gift—the miracle of healing. Amen.

O LORD my God, I called to you for help
   and you healed me. (PSALM 30:2)

Praise the LORD, my soul;
   all my inmost being, praise his holy name.
Praise the LORD, my soul,
   and forget not all his benefits—
who forgives all your sins
   and heals all your diseases,
who redeems your life from the pit
   and crowns you with love and compassion,
who satisfies your desires with good things
   so that your youth is renewed like the eagle's.
(PSALM 103:1–5)

I praise you because I am fearfully and wonderfully made. (PSALM 139:14a)

Thanks for My Pastor

Ministering Lord,

Thank You for my pastor, who bears Your holy word, who listens with concern, who prays with sympathy, who visits those in need, who administers absolution and the sacraments, who husbands the headstrong, who conducts meaningful worship, who conveys Your guidance, who shepherds souls. What a great gift is Your ambassador. May I honor his work and show him my appreciation. Sustain him in the challenges of his labors, keep his ministry faithful to Your word and will, and make him a blessing to those he serves. Amen.

"Keep watch over yourselves and all the flock of which the Holy Spirit has made you overseers. Be shepherds of the church of God, which he bought with his own blood." (Acts 20:28)

It was he who gave some to be apostles, some to be prophets, some to be evangelists, and some to be pastors and teachers, to prepare God's people for works of service, so that the body of Christ may be built up until we all reach unity in the faith and in the knowledge of the Son of God and become mature, attaining to the whole measure of the fullness of Christ. (Ephesians 4:11–13)

Thanks for Those Who Help and Pray

Beneficent Lord,

What blessing is the help of all those who surround me and tend to my care. Thank You for family, for close ones, for kind ones, for all those who have come to my aid in so many ways to ease my burdens, minister to my needs, and lift my spirits. How grateful I am for those who raise persistent prayers to You in my behalf. The unselfish and generous offerings of these dear ones restore me. I am consoled by their constancy and glad they are here. Praise to You, for they bear Your love and bring Your benediction. Amen.

For he will command his angels concerning you
    to guard you in all your ways. (PSALM 91:11)

Are not all angels ministering spirits sent to serve those who will inherit salvation? (HEBREWS 1:14)

PRAYERS OF CAREGIVERS

Nursing the Ill

Gentle Lord,

Work Your healing through me as I minister to the one in my care. Help me to apply my knowledge to make careful judgments. Guide my hands to competently perform my tasks. Give me strength to meet the challenges of the day, and patience to handle its demands. With clear, kind words, a gentle touch, and compassionate attention, help me to ease pain and fear. Forgive me when I have become hurried or curt under pressure. Make me dependable, but also dependent on You. Shine through my words and actions to reflect the light of Your glory with comfort and healing. Amen.

Praise be to the God and Father of our Lord Jesus Christ, the Father of compassion and the God of all comfort, who comforts us in all our troubles, so that we can comfort those in any trouble with the comfort we ourselves have received from God. (2 CORINTHIANS 1:3–4)

Responding to Needs

Comforting Lord,

Seeing my loved one ailing makes me frightened, hesitant, resentful, and sad. She/he likely feels these tremulous emotions, too. Teach me to accept the change in her/him and seek ways to respond to her/his needs. Help me to listen attentively to her/his wishes rather than imposing my will. I recognize that my own desires may need to be set aside for a time. Give me patient strength in this tedious and trying interlude. May I forgive myself when I fail to meet my own expectations. Let me be receptive to the unexpected blessings that our altered circumstances may reveal. Make me generous in encouragement and lavish in love. May my company be a comfort, my gaze a tender testament, and my touch a frequent grace. Amen.

For we are God's workmanship, created in Christ Jesus to do good works, which God prepared in advance for us to do. (EPHESIANS 2:10)

Encourage one another daily. (HEBREWS 3:13a)

Offering Help

Lord of Help,

I want to help, but I don't know how or what to do. Encourage me to overcome my timidity with personal acts of kindness. Help me to anticipate needs and to respond to them. Replace my vague offers of assistance with specific gestures to relieve a caregiver, shop for groceries, cook a meal, select a book, read a paper, answer mail, or return phone calls. I might run an errand, pick up prescriptions, drive to an appointment, accompany to treatment, or encourage through therapy. I can share a scripture, song, devotion, or prayer. Or I may simply sit and listen.

Prompt me to pay a visit, to pay attention. May I lift spirits with a positive and optimistic attitude. Thank You for showing me ways to serve and the blessings of service. Make me tireless in aid, persistent in prayer, and strong in faith. Through my small deeds, work Your healing. Amen.

———————————

If one falls down,
   a friend can help him up. (ECCLESIASTES 4:10a)

"She did what she could." (MARK 14:8a)

Each one should use whatever gift he has received to serve others, faithfully administering God's grace in its various forms. (1 PETER 4:10)

For Guidance

Guiding Lord,

Suddenly I have this overwhelming responsibility of care. I feel inadequate and unprepared. So much needs to be done. I don't know how to begin, and I don't see an end. Come to my side, and show me where to start. Assist me with making arrangements, setting priorities, establishing schedules, coordinating care. Help me to perform my obligations willingly and graciously. Spur my industry and diligence. Keep me mindful that the service I perform contributes to healing and comfort. May I labor in love, conscientious and cheerful, kind and courteous. Remind me that when prayers request Your help, the help You send may be me. Amen.

I will instruct you and teach you in the way you
    should go;
  I will counsel you and watch over you. (PSALM 32:8)

Trust in the LORD with all your heart
  and lean not on your own understanding;
in all your ways acknowledge him,
  and he will make your paths straight. (PROVERBS 3:5–6)

To Communicate

Word of God,

As giving and receiving care has shifted, our roles
have been redefined. Capabilities have changed, and
our relationship differs. Some responsibilities now in
my charge can mean confronting difficult, painful, or
sensitive issues. Addressing matters that we have not
previously discussed together can be uncomfortable. Give
me courage and tact in broaching these delicate subjects.
Let us welcome these imposed intimacies as opportunities
to develop new dimensions of our relationship. May
we learn to honestly convey our own needs, remaining
attentive to the other's desires. Show me how to offer
information, help, and guidance when needed, without
imposing my own will. May we always remember to
treat each other with courtesy, consideration, and respect.
Amen.

Serve one another in love. (GALATIANS 5:13c)

"Be sure to fear the LORD and serve him faithfully with all
your heart." (1 SAMUEL 12:24a)

Needing Help

Attentive Lord,

Caregiving is arduous work. Its responsibilities compound all those that already crowd my days. I seem always rushed and ever tired. Emotional turmoil exhausts me, too. In our changed circumstances, I share the frustration and discomfort of the one for whom I care. Help me to find the pace and balance that will best serve the needs of my dear one and myself. Remind me that I cannot offer my best when I am exhausted. Assist me in determining my limits and attending to my own health and well-being—taking a break, seeking a hand, adjusting commitments. Please provide solutions that will enable us all to thrive. Amen.

And my God will meet all your needs according to his glorious riches in Christ Jesus. (PHILIPPIANS 4:19)

Feeling Depressed

Compassionate Lord,
Life seems beyond my control, and I lose hope and heart. Relentless labors drain my body, diminish my mind, and depress my spirit. I have exhausted my own resources and wonder how I can continue. Relief eludes me, for responsibilities always remain on my mind. I need attention myself, but feel selfish for such desiring of it. May I lean on You, Lord? Your strength is dependable, Your companionship at hand in Your word. Sharing my burdens with You already eases them. Renew my energy, will, and optimism that I may cherish and tend this dear one You have entrusted to my care. Amen.

The LORD is close to the brokenhearted
and saves those who are crushed in spirit.
(PSALM 34:18)

"You will call, and the LORD will answer;
you will cry for help, and he will say: Here am I."
(ISAIAH 58:9)

His compassions never fail.
They are new every morning;
great is your faithfulness. (LAMENTATIONS 3:22b–23)

Assisting with Therapy

Conquering Lord,

Keep me mindful that the help I offer contributes to strengthening one of Yours in weakness. Help me to respect dignity in offering aid. May I be sensitive to personal concerns and needs to best assist in returning strength and function. Help me to understand how difficult it is to be dependent and to suggest manageable responsibilities, small though they may be. Fortify my own faith, spirit, and stamina. Make me persistent in praise and enthusiastic in encouragement. With cheer and optimism, may I prompt progress and inspire improvement. Through our efforts and Your power, we can conquer. Amen.

"By this kind of hard work we must help the weak, remembering the words the Lord Jesus himself said: 'It is more blessed to give than to receive.'" (ACTS 20:35)

Therefore encourage one another and build each other up, just as in fact you are doing. (1 THESSALONIANS 5:11)

In an Emergency

Loving Lord,
   This unexpected calamity has shaken me. My heart
is racing. I cannot seem to gather my thoughts. Clear
my mind that I may listen carefully, ask appropriate
questions, and make rational decisions. Give me a cool
head and a calm heart. Allay my own worries that I may
support and encourage my dear one(s). Strengthen me
to handle demands of the moment and to face whatever
challenges may be ahead. Assure us that in the midst
of this adversity, You are here, bearing us up whatever
befalls. Amen.

In his hand is the life of every creature and the breath of
all mankind. (JOB 12:10)

Hasten, O God, to save me;
   O Lord, come quickly to help me. (PSALM 70:1)

77

Caring for the Aging

Lord of the Ages,

Give me ease with the aging. Make me patient with slow minds, careful with frail limbs, clear to failing eyes and ears. Make me attentive to retold tales, available to help, ready to cheer with a smile. Make me sensitive to needs, respectful of dignity, and quick to wrap wrinkles with love. Amen.

"Honor your father and your mother." (EXODUS 20:12a)

"Rise in the presence of the aged, show respect for the elderly and revere your God. I am the LORD." (LEVITICUS 19:32)

When a Loved One Is Dying

My Heavenly Father,

How difficult it is to watch the life of my loved one ebb away. In my tears, I recall Your promises. But how hard it is to contemplate paradise while imagining earth without her/him. Help me through the pain of parting. Ease our farewells. May I recognize the benediction in these final times together, these last touches, closing words, and suspended smiles. Thank You for our shared and cherished memories, which assuage the anguish of anticipated absence. Make me attentive to my dear one and to Your grace. Release her/him gently to Your embrace. Amen.

He will swallow up death forever.
The Sovereign Lord will wipe away the tears from
    all faces. (Isaiah 25:8a)

"Surely I am with you always, to the very end of the age." (Matthew 28:20)

In Grief

Lord of Heaven,

And now it has come, that which we feared and evaded, dreaded and fought—the depth of loss we could not imagine, the profound quiet we now sense, the void we cannot yet completely conceive, the end that is only the beginning. We grieve that we could not keep our dear one near us longer, but rejoice that he/she will live in Your sweet company. In gratitude for the blessing shared in our life together, we commit (name) to Your loving grace. Console us with the steady stride of time, and comfort us with anticipation of our glorious reunion. Amen.

"Blessed are those who mourn,
for they will be comforted." (MATTHEW 5:4)

"You will grieve, but your grief will turn to joy."
(JOHN 16:20b)

"I tell you the truth, whoever hears my word and believes him who sent me has eternal life and will not be condemned; he has crossed over from death to life."
(JOHN 5:24)